LIGHTNING BOLT BOOKS™

Let's Visit the Tundra

Jennifer Boothroyd

Lerner Publications ✦ Minneapolis

For the
Neaton family

Lerner Publications Company
A division of Lerner Publishing Group, Inc.
241 First Avenue North
Minneapolis, MN 55401 USA

For reading levels and more information, look up this title at www.lernerbooks.com.

Library of Congress Cataloging-in-Publication Data

Names: Boothroyd, Jennifer, 1972– author.
Title: Let's visit the tundra / Jennifer Boothroyd.
Other titles: Let us visit the tundra
Description: Minneapolis : Lerner Publications, [2017] | Series: Lightning bolt books. Biome explorers | Audience: Ages 5–8. | Audience: K to grade 3. | Includes bibliographical references and index.
Identifiers: LCCN 2015047373 (print) | LCCN 2015049186 (ebook) | ISBN 9781512411966 (lb : alk. paper) | ISBN 9781512412345 (pb : alk. paper) | ISBN 9781512412048 (eb pdf)
Subjects: LCSH: Tundra ecology—Juvenile literature. | Tundra animals—Juvenile literature.
Classification: LCC QH541.5.T8 B66 2017 (print) | LCC QH541.5.T8 (ebook) | DDC 577.5/86—dc23
LC record available at http://lccn.loc.gov/2015047373

Manufactured in the United States of America
1-39750-21309-2/26/2016

Table of Contents

A Journey to the Tundra ... 4

Animals in the Tundra ... 10

Plants in the Tundra ... 17

Surviving Together ... 23

People in the Tundra ... 28

Biome Extremes ... 29

Glossary ... 30

Further Reading ... 31

Index ... 32

A Journey to the Tundra

Brrrr. A cold, dry wind blows across the tundra. The temperature here can be as cold as −30°F (−34°C). Winter in this biome can last for more than seven months.

Less than a foot (30 cm) of snow falls in the tundra in winter.

Parts of the tundra are covered by snow. But the tundra is very dry.

Much of the tundra stays frozen all year long. Soil that has been frozen for at least two years is called permafrost.

The tundra is found in far northern parts of the planet.

This map shows the arctic tundra biome. There is also an alpine tundra biome.

NORTH AMERICA

EUROPE

ASIA

AFRICA

SOUTH AMERICA

AUSTRALIA

Tundra

ANTARCTICA

The tundra looks very different in summer. The snow melts, and the topsoil thaws. Colorful wildflowers bloom.

Ponds form with water from melting snow. The warmer temperatures bring more animals and insects to the tundra.

Animals in the Tundra

Reindeer roam the tundra in large herds. They eat plants and lichens. Most reindeer migrate in winter. They move to find more food.

Arctic terns dive into the icy ocean to catch fish. As the weather gets colder, these birds fly south to the coast of Antarctica.

Many animals stay in the tundra all year. Hare, lemmings, foxes, and others grow white fur in winter. This helps them blend in with the snow. Their fur is gray or brown in summer.

This hare's white fur helps it blend in with the snow in winter.

Northern collared lemmings use their front claws to dig tunnels down to the permafrost. They eat plants and lichens.

An arctic fox has a bushy tail that helps it stay warm in its habitat. Arctic foxes follow polar bears. The foxes eat food the bears leave behind.

Arctic foxes also hunt lemmings.

Snowy owls listen for lemmings scurrying under the snow or grass. They also hunt small birds in midair.

A polar bear's thick webbed paws help it move on ice and in the water.

Polar bears hunt seals through ice on the Arctic Ocean. They live on land until the ice has frozen thick enough. Most polar bears can't find enough to eat on land and will travel very far to find food.

Plants in the Tundra

There are no trees in the tundra. Shrubs are the tallest plants. Arctic dwarf birch is a shrub. Its leaves turn red and orange in fall.

The prairie crocus has purple flowers. They open during the day and close at night.

The northern bog orchid is pollinated by mosquitoes. Pollinated flowers make seeds. The seeds grow into new flowers.

Lemmings eat many different plants in the tundra. They mix the soil when they dig burrows. This helps control the plant population.

Many animals such as ermines, owls, and foxes eat lemmings. When there are a lot of lemmings to eat, owls and ermines have more babies.

Ermines can hunt lemmings under the snow.

The foxes are hunted by wolves. Wolves also eat reindeer. If there were too many reindeer, they would eat more of the plants. Then smaller animals would not find enough to eat.

Each plant and animal in the tundra is very important to its survival!

People in the Tundra

Several groups of people have lived in the tundra for thousands of years, such as the Inuit people of Greenland and Canada. But not many people live in this biome. People here need to live and work responsibly. Pollution in other parts of the world is damaging the tundra. Pollution causes Earth to warm. Warmer temperatures will damage the tundra. People are working hard to stop pollution and control global warming.

Biome Extremes

- **Coldest tundra town:** Oymyakon, Russia (average yearly temperature 4°F, or −15°C, record −90°F, or −68°C)

- **Tundra town with longest winter night:** Longyearbyen, Norway, no sunrise for five months on average

- **Tundra town with longest summer day:** Longyearbyen, Norway, no sunset for five months on average

- **Largest tundra carnivore:** male polar bear, 8 to 9 feet (2.4 to 2.6 meters) from nose to tail, 1,320 to 1,760 pounds (600 to 800 kilograms)

- **Longest bird migration:** arctic terns, 44,000 miles (71,000 kilometers) a year

Glossary

biome: plants and animals in a large area, such as a desert or forest

ecosystem: an area of connected living and nonliving things

habitat: the natural home of a plant or animal

herd: a group of hoofed animals that stay together

lichen: a plantlike living creature that is a mix of algae and fungi

migrate: to move to another area when seasons change

pollinate: to carry seeds from one flower to make another flower

population: the number of living things in an area

shrub: a short, woody plant with many stems

surface: the uppermost layer of something

tundra: a large area of flat land that is always frozen and doesn't have trees

Further Reading

The Arctic
http://www.aitc.sk.ca/saskschools/arctic
/Aintro.html

Biomes of the World: Arctic Tundra
http://www.thewildclassroom.com/biomes
/arctictundra.html

Duke, Shirley. *Seasons of the Tundra Biome.* Vero Beach, FL: Rourke, 2013.

Felix, Rebecca. *What's Great about Alaska?* Minneapolis: Lerner Publications, 2016.

Fleisher, Paul. *Tundra Food Webs in Action.* Minneapolis: Lerner Publications, 2014.

World Biomes: Tundra
http://kids.nceas.ucsb.edu/biomes/tundra.html

Index

arctic dwarf birch, 17
arctic foxes, 14
arctic terns, 11, 29

cotton grass, 19

lemmings, 12–13, 15,
    24–25
lichens, 10, 13, 22

northern bog orchid, 21

polar bears, 14, 16, 29
prairie crocus, 20

reindeer, 10, 22, 26

snow, 5, 8–9, 12, 15
snowy owls, 15

Photo Acknowledgments

The images in this book are used with the permission of: © Cesar Ed/Science Source/
Getty Images, pp. 2, 25; © Jason Edwards/National Geographic/Getty Images, p. 4;
© Pattyn/blickwinkel/Alamy, p. 5; © WILDLIFE GmbH/Alamy, p. 6; © Laura Westlund/
Independent Picture Service, p. 7; © Danilo Forcellini/Alamy, p. 8; © Brian Kennedy/
Moment Open/Getty Images, p. 9; © Donald M. Jones/Minden Pictures/Getty Images,
p. 10; © Darrell Gulin/Photodisc/Getty Images, p. 11; © NULL/FLPA/Alamy, p. 12;
© Wayne Lynch/All Canada Photos/Getty Images, pp. 13, 17, 22; © David W. Hamilton/
The Image Bank/Getty Images, p. 14; © Todd Ryburn Photography/Moment/Getty
Images, p. 15; © Wolfgang Kaehler/LightRocket/Getty Images, p. 16; © Matthias
Breiter/Minden Pictures/Getty Images, p. 18; © Michael S. Quinton/National
Geographic Creative/Alamy, pp. 19, 23; © iStockphoto.com/Ssvyat, pp. 20, 31; © Colin
Varndell/Minden Pictures, p. 21; © Andrey Zvoznikov/ardea.com/Pantheon/SuperStock,
p. 24; © Josef Pittner/iStock/Thinkstock, p. 26; © Robert Postma/Design Pics/First
Light/Getty Images, p. 27.

Front cover: © Tt/Dreamstime.com.

Main body text set in Johann Light 30/36.